ASTROLOGY

ASTROLOGY

A Guide to the Signs

Ariel Books

Andrews and McMeel

Kansas City

10 9 8 7 6

ISBN: 0-8362-3014-0

Library of Congress Catalog Card Number: 91-77095

Marbleized endpapers © 1985 Katherine Radcliffe
Design: Diane Stevenson / SNAP • HAUS GRAPHICS

INTRODUCTION

The oldest existing astrological charts date from 400 B.C., from the area of the world known then as Babylonia. But the technique was old even then. Astrology predates recorded history.

Long ago, when Man and Woman first looked into the night sky in order to understand their place in the universe, they began to perceive shifts and changes over the course of the year. Certain patterns began to emerge. Early humankind recognized that some objects were fixed in the sky, while others seemed to move in strange paths, sometimes even moving backward in the sky.

The most special objects became known as

planets. And until the Renaissance—when scientific theories were developed to explain their odd movements—planets held a mystical fascination for watchers of the sky. Their erratic movements held an inexplicable magic.

Astrologers gradually began to piece these patterns together into a system of divination. The zodiac, a circular belt of sky that circles the earth, was divided into twelve zones. Each zone became a different "sign," and was associated with different characteristics.

When we talk about astrological signs, we are speaking specifically of the different sun signs—that is, which zone of the zodiac the sun was in at the time of one's birth. (For example, between the 22nd of January and the 21st of February, the sun is in the sign of

Aquarius. Those born between those dates are born in that sun sign.)

The twelve different zones of the zodiac are composed of different elements and qualities. The four elements are Fire, Earth, Air, and Water. Fire is creative; Earth, materialistic; Air, intellectual and abstract; and Water, emotional. Blended with these elements are three qualities: Cardinal, Fixed, and Mutable. The Cardinal quality is aggressive and the mark of a leader. A Fixed quality has stability. A Mutable quality gives the talent of change and adaptability.

Each sign is a different combination of an element and a quality. For example, Aries combines the Fire element with the Cardinal quality, indicating a strong, creative leader.

Each zodiacal sign also became associated with different parts of the body, which often relate to the symbol of each zone. (For example, Taurus rules the neck and throat. Those born under this sign often have prominent, thick necks, like bulls.)

The sun sign is only one aspect of a person's personality. While it is one of the strongest personality indicators, there are many other influences. The moon has a very strong influence. Since it changes its relative position in the sky more quickly, one's moon sign can be very different from one's sun sign. The ascendant (the point at which the horizon intersects with the zodiac at the time of one's birth) has a strong effect on the whole astrological chart. Beyond that, the positions of the different planets at the time of one's birth each contribute to the whole environment.

Of those planets, Mercury, the mythological messenger of the gods, deals with communication. Mercury is close to the sun and usually shares the same zone. If it doesn't, it's usually in an adjacent sign. Its position can determine how one thinks and shares those thoughts with others.

Venus was the goddess of love. Her planet deals with passive elements of love and sexuality. Its position in a chart can point out where one finds physical pleasure and fulfillment.

Mars is the ruler of active sexuality. In mythology, Mars was the god of war, and this planet reflects positive force and aggression. In some signs, this planet may point to a forceful, outgoing personality; Mars may be tempered in the more passive zodiacal zones like Cancer or Pisces.

Jupiter rules the outside world, how one views it, and one's place in it. This planet has a great deal to do with one's luck, justice, fate, and other determining issues of life.

Saturn has an even greater effect on fate, especially as it determines one's social status and restrictions. Every twenty-eight years or so, Saturn returns to where it was placed in the sky when one was born. Those times can produce great stress in one's life and mark major turning points.

The outer planets, Uranus, Neptune, and Pluto, have more to do with groups of people than with individuals. They take years to move from one sign to another and their influence can span generations. In general, Uranus deals with new ideas and new technologies; Neptune rules fashion and may help explain why one look can be in one year and out the next; Pluto deals with the subconscious, underground movements and revolutions, death and rebirth.

While we usually think of people having astrological signs, anything that has a moment of creation can have its own chart—a partnership, a building, an organization or institution. The United States was born on July 4, 1776, making it a Cancer. Consider the Cancerian aspects of this country: We have an almost mystical reverence for motherhood (Cancer's ruling planet, the moon, is symbol of the mother) and a strong empathy for the underdog. When we go to war, it's necessary for us to be persuaded that it's because an aggressor has taken advantage of a weaker country.

While the sun sign is the strongest influence on our astrological being, it is worthwhile to find out the positions of all the planets and create complete astrological charts for ourselves, friends, and loved ones. It can help us to better understand one another, realize what motivates us to act in certain ways, and help us appreciate the amazing diversity of our collective human experience.

ARIES

THE RAM

March 21–April 20

Aries is the first sign of the zodiac. Those born under the ram are creative and daring, the first to venture into new lands or new careers. This is the sign of trailblazers and pioneers.

Like the ram, those born under this fire sign are headstrong, forceful, and impulsive. Impulsiveness can lead to trouble, but Aries soon gets up, does a little brushing off, and moves on to the next adventure.

Ruling Planet: Mars
Element: Fire
Quality: Positive; masculine
First Desire: To lead
Day: Sunday
Body Part: Head
Foods: Leeks, shallots, cayenne pepper,
  spicy dishes
Animals: Sheep, rams
Color: Red
Jewels: Amethyst, diamond
Metal: Iron
Plants: Thistle, byrony
Flower: Honeysuckle
Magical Number: 5
Key Words: Enthusiastic, youthful,
  hopeful, selfish

Aries • A short, spectacular relationship. Two Aries can work up a lot of fireworks. But when they clash—and they will before long—the battles will be horrific.

Taurus • Can be a productive combination. Aries may get impatient with Taurus's practicality, but, if heeded, the bull can help focus the ram's creativity to more fruitful ends.

Gemini • The main attraction in this relationship will be Gemini's famous wit. These two may soon move on to other interests, but their parting will be friendly.

Cancer • A difficult combination. Aries has trouble putting up with Cancer's moodiness and can, in a thoughtless moment, inflict deep wounds to the sensitive crab.

Leo • This relationship takes a lot of work on both sides. Aries must remember to give Leo enough praise. Leo must in turn bow to Aries's lead. The rewards are worth the effort.

Virgo • This relationship has potential, but takes effort. Aries can provide some needed creativity and imagination, but will need to learn to be patient with the cautious Virgo.

Libra • This relationship will burn itself out quickly. Physically, the two are compatible, but Aries cannot shrug off an argument the way Libra can.

Scorpio • An extremely hard relationship. Both have great energy and are likely to be attracted. But Scorpio's attempts to dominate might cause the ram to bolt.

Sagittarius • A good combination. These two are both mentally and physically compatible. Each will find the other an exciting and good-humored companion.

Capricorn • A difficult, but sometimes rewarding combination. Aries can help cautious Capricorn break out of that rut. Capricorn has the practicality to make some of Aries's wildest schemes come true.

Aquarius • A very compatible relationship. Aries may find Aquarius inattentive, but with understanding, these two will click and share many new and exciting experiences together.

Pisces • A complex relationship. Pisces's uncanny intuition can be fascinating. Aries will have to learn to think ahead a little. One careless remark can leave Pisces brooding for days.

TAURUS

THE BULL

April 21–May 21

Taurus is symbolized by the bull. This sign is marked by a cautious nature. Those born under this earth sign plow ahead at a comfortable pace, knowing that the race is not to the swift, but to the steady.

Those born under the bull are affectionate and loving. They may seem possessed of infinite patience, but be careful. Once that patience is tried beyond its limits, Taurus can explode with a fury that is intense. Think of a volcano; for centuries it may lie dormant, but inside the pressure constantly builds. If the pressure is too great, it will erupt and wreak great destruction.

Ruling Planet: Venus
Element: Earth
Quality: Negative; feminine
First Desire: Stability
Day: Friday
Body Parts: Throat and neck
Foods: Wheat, berries, apples, pears, grapes, asparagus
Animals: Cattle
Color: Pink
Jewels: Emerald, moss agate
Metal: Copper
Plants: Daisy moss, spinach
Flowers: Rose, poppy, foxglove
Magical Number: 6
Key Words: Stable, patient, secure, stubborn

TAURUS AND . . .

Aries • A difficult relationship, with some potential. Taurus will have to let the ram take the lead to keep the relationship harmonious.

Taurus • These two will enjoy long walks and sensuous dinners together. Both will be stubborn in disagreements and may need an outside mediator.

Gemini • Taurus can have trouble leaving the trodden path. Gemini offers new experiences and perspectives. This relationship probably will not last, but it will give Taurus some needed variety.

Cancer • Cancer is impressed by Taurus's strength and loves to take things slowly. This relationship may last forever.

Leo • While these two may be affectionate, they will differ on money issues. Leo likes to spend money and Taurus doesn't.

Virgo • Taurus and Virgo can make a very comfortable relationship. Both these earth signs like to stake out their ground and may need to do a little negotiating before they can settle down.

Libra • While Libra prefers the abstract, Taurus loves the sensual. This combination can work, but it takes much effort from both partners. Jealousy may wreck the relationship.

Scorpio • Taurus prefers safety, Scorpio loves danger. But the attraction between the two is powerful. Together, they may encounter worlds they never knew existed.

Sagittarius • An affair or friendship can be stimulating, but a marriage will strain Taurus's patience. Sagittarius is just too free a spirit to stay in one place for long.

Capricorn • A very pleasant and comfortable relationship. Capricorn respects Taurus's determination and they will usually agree on money matters. (That is, they will agree that money matters!)

Aquarius • Aquarius is an agreeable and stimulating companion. But Taurus will be sadly disappointed with the results of any relationship deeper than a casual acquaintance.

Pisces • These two people share a deep emotional nature. Taurus may be bewildered, though, at Pisces's chaotic feelings. A little patience will help them weather the storms.

GEMINI

THE TWINS

May 22–June 21

Gemini is the sign of the twins, and a certain duality always marks it. A Gemini may seem possessed of conflicting personalities, now affectionate and fun-filled, then suddenly cold and impersonal.

Gemini is a restless air sign, more comfortable with change and constant stimulation than security. Those born under this sign like to travel and to meet new experiences. Their quick wit makes them immediately attractive, but their restlessness may make it hard for them to form long-lasting relationships.

Ruling Planet: Mercury

Element: Air

Quality: Positive; masculine

First Desire: To communicate

Day: Wednesday

Body Parts: Shoulders, arms, nerves

Foods: Nuts, beans, peas, carrots

Animals: Small birds, butterflies, monkeys

Color: Yellow

Jewels: Aquamarine, beryl

Metal: Mercury

Plants: Ferns, myrtle

Flowers: Honeysuckle, jasmine

Magical Number: 7

Key Words: Witty, superficial, forthright, quick

GEMINI AND . . .

Aries • Love can quickly blossom between these two, and just as quickly fade. But after the initial attraction, they will remain good friends and share many laughs.

Taurus • Taurus prefers the known, the reliable, the proven. Gemini needs to experiment and discover new ideas, new people. Gemini will soon become bored with the steady bull.

Gemini • One Gemini is already enough personality for two people; imagine twice that! The relationship between these two will be exciting, but it cannot sustain itself for long.

Cancer • Gemini loves to play, but Cancer insists on taking things seriously. Gemini wants to greet new experiences, Cancer's typical mode is retreat. This relationship is short and unhappy.

Leo • A good combination. Leo will be attracted by Gemini's charm and is independent enough to let Gemini wander occasionally.

Virgo • Virgo demands a controlled routine, which restricts Gemini unmercifully. Eventually Gemini will move on to a more congenial partner.

Libra • An intellectual and thrilling combination. Gemini and Libra often think alike. Any disagreements they have will be more stimulating than divisive.

Scorpio • These two may be very attracted at first, but their personalities clash. Scorpio can be very jealous. The Scorpio-Gemini combination that lasts is rare indeed.

Sagittarius • These two share a carefree approach to the world and will enjoy each other immensely. Their only problem will be getting their calendars together for appointments—and then remembering to show up.

Capricorn • Capricorn has trouble understanding Gemini's restless nature. The goat isn't interested in discovery, just in getting ahead. A long-term relationship is unlikely.

Aquarius • A pleasurable combination. Each instinctively understands the other's needs and can accommodate them. There may not be fireworks, but a friendship or even a marriage will last.

Pisces • Initially these two share the quality of mutability and find each other sympathetic. But Pisces's emotional demands will irk Gemini. This relationship cannot hold for long.

CANCER

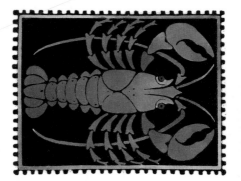

THE CRAB

June 22–July 23

Cancer is the sign of the crab, which sounds like an insult. It's not. Think of the soft inner body of a crab, surrounded by a thin, brittle shell. That's the image of a Cancer. A soft inner soul, protected by a thin shell.

Cancers are loyal and very empathetic. They will be the first to notice if a friend or a relative needs a hug. But their sensitivity costs them. Cancers are quick to feel a hurt and once that thin shell is penetrated, they are helpless to protect themselves.

Ruling Planet: The Moon
Element: Water
Quality: Feminine
First Desire: Security
Day: Monday
Body Parts: Chest, breasts
Foods: Turnips, cabbage, milk
Animals: Creatures with a shell
Color: Violet
Jewel: Emerald
Metal: Silver
Plant: Hazelnut tree
Flowers: Geranium, water lily, other white flowers
Magical Number: 2
Key Words: Moody, kind, sympathetic, controlled, disciplined

Aries • Aries has a strong attraction for Cancer, but the relationship may not last long. One thoughtless remark from Aries can deeply wound the sensitive crab.

Taurus • Both these signs favor home activities and enjoy themselves there to the exclusion of the rest of the world. Cancer's imagination can keep this relationship from becoming boring.

Gemini • Geminis are possessed of charm and wit. But after a while, Cancer will realize that that charm is nonexclusive. Most Geminis cannot give the undivided attention that Cancer desires.

Cancer • A complex, long-lasting relationship. Excessive sensitivity by both could cause turbulence in the relationship. Fights will be made up quickly, but not forgotten.

Leo • This combination can be a winner. The outgoing lion is just what the crab needs to open up that shell. Leo's charm can go a long way toward satisfying Cancer's need for affection.

Virgo • While Virgos can seem cold and demanding, Cancers have a way of bringing out their warm, affectionate side. Petty quarrels could impede the relationship, however.

Libra • A difficult combination. Both are uncomfortable making decisions and Libra's emotional detachment can leave Cancer feeling even more insecure.

Scorpio • This combination is deep and lasting. Scorpio provides the protection Cancer needs. Cancer instinctively understands the passion under the still exterior of Scorpio.

Sagittarius • A better friendship than a marriage. Sagittarius's free and easy ways are sure to excite Cancerian jealousy.

Capricorn • A difficult relationship. Capricorn's practicality may put a damper on Cancer's imagination. But Cancer can help bring out those passions buried deep under Capricorn's tough hide.

Aquarius • Cancer lives by intuition; Aquarius thrives on logic. These two will never see eye to eye and the relationship will be marked by emotional storms.

Pisces • A very compatible combination. Both these signs are deeply emotional and imaginative. However, they are both subject to sudden depressions and dark moods.

LEO

THE LION

July 24–August 23

Leo the lion is the sun child of the zodiac. Those born under this fire sign have winning, outgoing personalities. They respond to attention the way a cat responds to a good scratch behind the ears. But withhold your admiration and watch the claws come out!

But why withhold it? Leos shine in any crowd. And they can give as good as they get. When you receive a smile from the regal Leo, you'll feel as if the sun's just come out after a long, wet rain.

Ruling Planet: The Sun
Element: Fire
Quality: Positive; masculine
First Desire: Power
Day: Sunday
Body Parts: Heart, spine, back
Foods: Rice, honey, meat
Animals: Lions, tigers
Colors: Red, orange, gold, yellow
Jewels: Amber, ruby, chrysolite
Metal: Gold
Tree: Oak
Flowers: Sunflower, marigold
Magical Number: 19
Key Words: Creative, sensitive, bossy

Aries • These two will certainly create a lot of sparks. Fire signs have healthy egos and when they clash, all innocent bystanders should take cover.

Taurus • A relationship with potential. Taurus is attracted to Leo's warmth, but the lion's extravagance could spark conflict.

Gemini • A good combination. Charming, entertaining Gemini amuses Leo and is not about to defy the natural authority of the lion.

Cancer • A promising combination. Cancer's vulnerability can be irresistible and with the loyal crab, Leo won't have to look any further for attention.

Leo • A strong combination, but can there be two brightest stars in the heavens? These two will have to learn to share the spotlight.

Virgo • This relationship will have difficulties. Leo is all warmth, while Virgo is cool. This combination is like fire and ice.

Libra • Leo might find Libra a little too honest for comfort, but otherwise this combination is electrifying.

Scorpio • An interesting combination. Scorpio and Leo can open each other up to whole new experiences. But beware of power struggles.

Sagittarius • A good, short-term relationship. These two will love sharing adventures. But Leo will eventually want to settle down, and Sagittarius never will.

Capricorn • Capricorns are too future-oriented to enjoy the present. Eventually Leo will find this relationship depressing.

Aquarius • Aquarius's unorthodox ideas are stimulating, but the Water Bearer's endless analyzing can drive Leo up the wall.

Pisces • A difficult combination. Leo is just plain mystified by Pisces's emotional instability and martyr complex.

VIRGO

THE VIRGIN

August 24–September 23

The sixth sign of the zodiac, Virgo is symbolized by the Virgin. Virgos have a strong sense of self and of moral and ethical conduct. Their homes are always clean and tidy. Their clothes are always well-kept and good-fitting.

Many Virgos are especially good at communication. They choose their words with precision. And when they say "no," the meaning is clear. Virgos may sometimes seem overly critical and demanding. But there is no one better to have around in times of adversity, when they are both capable and kind.

Ruling Planet: Mercury
Element: Earth
Quality: Negative; feminine
First Desire: Crystallization
Day: Wednesday
Body Parts: Stomach, intestines
Foods: Carrots, potatoes, vegetables grown under the soil
Animals: Cats, dogs
Color: Brown
Jewels: Cobblestone, emerald, jasper
Metals: Nickel, mercury
Tree: Apple
Flowers: Buttercup, forget-me-not
Magical Number: 7
Key Words: Practical, critical, anxious, intelligent

Aries • An enlightening relationship for both. Aries can teach Virgo to loosen up a little. Virgo can encourage Aries to think ahead.

Taurus • A good combination. The bull may be a little clumsy and sloppy for Virgo, but they'll have a comfortable, easy time together.

Gemini • An unhappy marriage. Virgo will be appalled at Gemini's irresponsibility and lack of structure. Gemini will be offended at Virgo's criticisms.

Cancer • A very good combination. Virgo will have to learn to make suggestions in a more sensitive manner to avoid conflict. But otherwise, these two are sympathetic to each other.

Leo • A difficult combination. Leo's constant need for attention will annoy Virgo, whose own virtues often get overlooked. These two also have vastly different attitudes toward money.

Virgo • Both will be quick to point out the flaws in the other. But mutual interests will keep this pair together.

Libra • Intellectual disagreements will be stimulating. Emotionally, this combination will be very challenging.

Scorpio • An interesting combination. Virgo will need to relax some control to truly appreciate the virtues of Scorpio. But once that happens, the relationship will only deepen.

Sagittarius • A short-term relationship. Sagittarius can help Virgo look at the big picture, but any relationship between the two will not last.

Capricorn • Both are earth signs and share a longing for the practical and material. They may need to cultivate outside interests to avoid boredom.

Aquarius • Aquarius can open Virgo up to new experiences. But once the novelty wears off, there is not much left to the relationship.

Pisces • Patience is needed, although Pisces and Virgo can teach each other much. Virgo can provide stability for the chaotic fish, while Pisces can open Virgo up to the more irrational aspects of the world.

LIBRA

THE SCALES

September 24–October 23

Balance. Harmony. These are the attributes of those born under the sign of the scales. But the scales do not always balance easily. Libras are subject to extreme swings in their quest to achieve equilibrium.

Libras are often farsighted and original thinkers. They are natural leaders and are likely to be found in the all-night coffee houses, plotting the next revolution. But don't worry. For these air signs, the discussion is far more important than the actual execution.

Ruling Planet: Venus
Element: Air
Quality: Masculine
First Desire: Union
Day: Friday
Body Part: Kidneys
Foods: Wheats and cereals, berries, apples, pears, grapes
Animals: Reptiles
Color: Indigo
Jewels: Diamond, opal
Metal: Copper
Trees: Ash, poplar
Flower: Rose
Magical Number: 3
Key Words: Diplomatic, fair, charming, aggressive

Aries • These two can be quickly attracted—and just as quickly repulsed. Power struggles will be an issue. Both Aries and Libra are cardinal signs and like to take the lead.

Taurus • A strong and stormy combination. Libra provides the originality, and Taurus the power, to change the world. But both will need to compromise their thinking to stay together.

Gemini • Gemini is fascinating, but Libra may be disappointed to discover there's not much substance behind the twin sign's witticisms.

Cancer • Cancer may not come up to Libra's standards—too emotional, too sticky. A long relationship will take patience and determination from both.

Leo • A fiery relationship. The attraction between these two can be irresistible, but in a clash of wills, Libra will need to yield.

Virgo • Libra will have trouble understanding Virgo's stay-at-home attitude and stinginess. A long-lasting combination is unlikely.

Libra • These two will have much in common, but may have a difficult time settling down to any kind of commitment. A lasting relationship will take work from both.

Scorpio • A volatile combination. Scorpio's explosive jealousy can be exacerbated by Libra's free and easy social manners.

Sagittarius • A good combination. Sagittarius needs to wander freely. Libra is one of the few signs able to tolerate that kind of freedom—as long as Sagittarius manages to get home once in a while.

Capricorn • With a common goal, these two are a strong combination, but Libra may be shocked at Capricorn's "win at all costs" attitude.

Aquarius • A good combination. This relationship may not follow the rules, but it can last and will provide thrills for both.

Pisces • A frustrating relationship. Pisces cannot provide the direction Libra needs. These two may find their relationship going around and around in circles.

SCORPIO

THE SCORPION

October 24–November 22

Scorpio is both fixed and a water sign. Scorpio is the proverbial still water that runs deep. On the surface, Scorpios will appear tranquil, but dark emotions run turbulent underneath. Because of this, they are at their best during a crisis.

Scorpios often possess magnetic personalities, especially for the opposite sex. They make passionate lovers and good marriage partners. There are always new depths to discover with Scorpios. But beware, they are not casual lovers. The Scorpio possesses a jealous streak and an everlasting capacity for revenge.

Ruling Planets: Pluto; Mars
Element: Water
Quality: Feminine
First Desire: Control
Day: Tuesday
Body Part: Genitals
Foods: Onions, cayenne peppers, spicy foods
Animals: Insects, other invertebrates
Colors: Black, purple
Jewels: Amethyst, cinnabar, topaz
Metals: Steel, iron
Plants: Brambleberry, heather
Flowers: Geranium, honeysuckle
Magical Number: 4
Key Words: Passionate, energetic, warm, jealous

Aries • A difficult combination. Aries can be an irresistible force and Scorpio an immovable object. Unless one is willing to yield, this relationship can come to a grinding halt.

Taurus • A good combination. Taurus may seem dull and plodding to others, but Scorpio finds the pace just fine. These two share a deep attraction.

Gemini • A difficult combination. Gemini can be exciting but is so fickle that Scorpio's deep-rooted jealousy can be aroused, sometimes with disastrous results.

Cancer • For the most part, Cancer and Scorpio are sympathetic and well-matched. But these two don't take anything lightly. Their few clashes will leave deep scars.

Leo • Sunny Leo can help Scorpio shake off those dark spells. But any attempts to possess or manipulate the lion will backfire. Disputes can easily turn physical. A long-term relationship is a risky proposition.

Virgo • Not a long-lasting relationship. Virgo's critical eye will find all the faults in Scorpio, which will agonize the sensitive water sign. Scorpio will be put off by the detachment that Virgo displays.

Libra • Any relationship between these two will be stormy. Libra will want to socialize much more often than Scorpio will. There may be disagreements about money.

Scorpio • This combination is marked by extreme highs and lows. If these two present each other with their best, the Scorpion passion and loyalty, this relationship can work well. The danger is, they might just bring out the worst in each other.

Sagittarius • An extremely short-lived relationship. A little bit of Sagittarius is a welcome change, but not even Scorpio can keep this sign in one place.

Capricorn • Can be a good combination, with patience on both sides. Scorpio can dig out those well-hidden Capricorn virtues, and the goat is the type that stays put, which can quiet that famous Scorpio jealousy.

Aquarius • A short-term relationship. Aquarius loves a crowd; Scorpio wants to stay home. Eventually these two will part ways.

Pisces • A perfect match. These two water signs find each other emotionally compatible. Pisces will gladly follow Scorpio's lead.

SAGITTARIUS

THE ARCHER
November 23–December 21

The symbol of Sagittarius is the archer. He is usually depicted as part horse with his bow raised high and his head up. The image fits. Sagittarius is always looking up to see the bright, sunny side. Those born under this fire sign are highly creative, funny, and very attractive.

They're not very practical. But who cares? Sagittarius loves to travel, and is too busy sampling the exotic pleasures of the world to worry about earthly concerns. Just don't wait for those born under this sign to settle down. They never will.

Ruling Planet: Jupiter
Element: Fire
Quality: Positive; masculine
First Desire: Liberty
Day: Thursday
Body Parts: Hips, thighs, liver
Foods: Grapefruit, raisins, bulb vegetables
Animals: Deer, other hunted creatures
Color: Light blue
Jewel: Turquoise
Metal: Tin
Trees: Lime, birch
Flowers: Begonia, dandelion, carnation
Magical Number: 6
Key Words: Enthusiastic, optimistic, philosophical, restless

Aries • This relationship can be both lasting and satisfying. Both these fire signs need change and novelty and can provide it for each other.

Taurus • A frustrating relationship. Sagittarius will chafe at Taurus's plodding pace. Taurus, who takes everything seriously, will have trouble accepting Sagittarius's carefree attitude.

Gemini • These two are blessed with endless energy. But it may be difficult to channel all that energy in any definite direction. Eventually they may just drift apart.

Cancer • These two make better friends than lovers. Sagittarius will find the crab too sensitive for comfort and can take Cancer's insecurity for only so long.

Leo • A good combination. Sagittarius will appreciate the independence of Leo, who is not afraid to let the archer wander. Also, Leo is interesting enough to keep Sagittarius coming back for more.

Virgo • A relationship with both problems and potential. If Sagittarius can live with Virgo's set and boring routines, this earth sign can provide the purpose the archer often lacks.

Libra • Libra is a stimulating, intellectual companion, whose attitudes mesh well with those of Sagittarius. Libra can provide a little needed polish for the happy-go-lucky Sagittarius.

Scorpio • Sagittarius should beware of this relationship. The archer doesn't like to go in too far, and Scorpio is very deep water indeed. Sagittarius could get in over his or her head.

Sagittarius • Two archers will find each other great companions. But, with all their other interests, they will need to make time for each other.

Capricorn • A difficult relationship. Sagittarius may initially admire Capricorn's practicality, but living with it is something else.

Aquarius • A good combination. Their relationship may start out as a good friendship and deepen into something more.

Pisces • A confusing relationship. Both are mutable signs, which means they can adapt instantly to new situations. But neither can provide the stability they really crave.

CAPRICORN

THE GOAT

December 22–January 20

Capricorn the goat often follows a rocky path. But since Capricorn is thinking about the goal and not the road, those born under this sign can weather the hard spots. Their main problem is learning to smell the roses along the way.

Although Capricorns seem tough and stubborn, they are surprisingly sensitive. A careless remark can leave them brooding for days. They can't shrug things off the way some more sunny signs can. But still, they manage to persevere and often excel. Capricorns aren't content until they've climbed the peaks to heights of glory.

Ruling Planet: Saturn
Element: Earth
Quality: Negative; feminine
First Desire: Attainment
Day: Wednesday
Body Part: Knees, skin, bones, teeth
Foods: Pasta, meat, barley, starchy foods
Animals: Goats, cloven-footed creatures
Colors: Charcoal gray, black, green
Jewel: Emerald
Metal: Silver
Tree: Apple
Flowers: Ivy, pansy, amaranthus
Magical Number: 4
Key Words: Outgoing, forthright, level-
   headed, aloof

Aries • Conflict can be an overriding factor in this relationship. These two will clash often. Mellowing on both their parts can help create a positive relationship.

Taurus • These two earth signs have a lot in common—a need for security, a love of home, a respect for money. This combination can be a winner.

Gemini • A long-term relationship is unlikely. Gemini's changeable nature is liable to bewilder the steadier goat.

Cancer • A difficult relationship. Cancer's bouts of self-pity can exasperate Capricorn. But with sensitivity on Capricorn's part, this combination can work.

Leo • A short-term relationship. Capricorn will be frustrated at all the attention Leo demands when there are more important things for the goat to think about.

Virgo • These two signs are very compatible. While others may find Virgo critical, Capricorn can appreciate the earth sign's practicality and good sense. These two can help each other shed inhibitions and can even become affectionate together.

Libra • These two may be attracted at first, but without a common goal, the relationship will not last. Capricorn will find Libra's lack of commitment unsatisfying.

Scorpio • This relationship can work well with compromises from both sides. Capricorn may need to curb those ambitions to make sure that the future includes a lot of Scorpio.

Sagittarius • An unwise combination. Capricorn will resent Sagittarius's needs to spend time with other people.

Capricorn • Not an exciting relationship, but one that can last. Both regard life and career as very serious, and will share common priorities. Outside interests can help this relationship from becoming too boring.

Aquarius • This relationship will take a lot of work. Aquarius and Capricorn view life differently. Capricorn may mistake Aquarius's unconventional outlook for foolishness.

Pisces • A complex relationship. Sometimes these two will share wonderful moments of intimacy and love. But Pisces's sudden changes will confuse Capricorn.

AQUARIUS

THE WATER BEARER

January 21–February 19

To the casual observer, those born under the sign of the Water Bearer may seem, well, not quite normal. This air sign is marked by genius, unorthodox behavior, and sometimes just plain weirdness. They may seem like visitors from the future—or another planet.

Aquarians are acute thinkers, coming up with ideas of real genius, often ahead of their time. They can become fixated, however, and turn more stubborn than any Taurus. But, like all air signs, they are quite sociable. It's possible for them to retain friendships even with those with whom they disagree deeply.

Ruling Planet: Uranus
Element: Air
Quality: Masculine
First Desire: To know and understand
Day: Saturday
Body Part: Shins, ankles
Foods: Dried fruits, frozen foods
Animals: Eagles, large birds
Colors: All colors of the spectrum
Jewel: Opal
Metal: Aluminum
Plant: Myrrh
Flower: Orchid
Magical Number: 22
Key Words: Eccentric, friendly, glamorous, unpredictable

Aries • A very compatible relationship. These two share a common approach to life, even though Aries is self-centered and Aquarius is just the opposite. Aquarius will just laugh off Aries's attempt to dominate.

Taurus • Both are strong-willed people. But Taurus is likely to be looking for a deeper relationship than Aquarius. A long-term relationship will cause frustration.

Gemini • A stimulating combination. Aquarius will find in Gemini an exciting and amusing partner, especially in conversation. Whether the relationship ends soon, or lasts, both will enjoy the other's company.

Cancer • Aquarius would do well to steer away from the crab. Cancer takes things far too seriously for the casual Water Bearer and will put a definite crimp in that busy schedule.

Leo • These two may be quickly attracted to each other, but they are in for horrendous conflicts. Aquarius is bound to resent Leo's domineering ways, while Leo will start to growl at Aquarius's seeming indifference.

Virgo • This relationship can last on an intellectual level. Anything other than that will run into trouble. Virgo and Aquarius have completely different ideas of proper behavior.

Libra • A great combination. Aquarius and Libra share an unconventional approach to life. Libra, specifically, has a playfulness that Aquarius appreciates.

Scorpio • An unhappy combination. Scorpio's natural jealousy will be inflamed by Aquarius's need for social contact. The relationship could turn very ugly.

Sagittarius • An excellent combination. Aquarius may have to develop even more creativity to keep up with Sagittarius. But both are fun-loving, independent companions.

Capricorn • A difficult combination. Capricorn approaches everything with caution, which will hamper Aquarius's style. There may be fights over money.

Aquarius • A very pleasant combination. These two may seem to lack warmth to others, but their casual approach will please each other. In the best relationship, these two will have many mutual interests.

Pisces • A complex and difficult relationship. There are bound to be mixed signals and misunderstandings in this relationship.

PISCES

THE FISH

February 20–March 20

As the last sign in the zodiac, Pisces embodies the highest ideals of mankind—spirituality, sensitivity, self-sacrifice. Those born under the sign of the fish are unworldly, caring, and giving, especially of their hearts.

They can also be demanding emotionally. Pisceans are driven by the emotional chaos of their element of water. Their sudden mood changes can seem bewildering. But still there is always something very compelling about the fish, particularly in the eyes. One look from a Pisces can melt even the stoniest of hearts.

Ruling Planet: Neptune
Element: Water
Quality: Feminine
First Desire: Unification
Day: Thursday
Body Part: Feet
Food: Cucumbers, pumpkin, melon
Animals: Fish
Color: Aquamarine
Jewel: Chrysolite
Metal: Platinum, tin
Plants: Seaweed, moss
Flower: Water lily
Magical Number: 11
Key Words: Spiritual, reclusive, sensitive, inspired

Aries • A combination with possibilities. Pisces will appreciate Aries's strong lead. Give-and-take is essential to a successful relationship between these two.

Taurus • An iffy combination. Pisces will need to decide early on whether to pursue the relationship, as once Taurus is entrenched, it's impossible to get rid of the bull.

Gemini • A short-term relationship can be great. But Gemini is changeable, especially where relationships are concerned. The good times will not last long.

Cancer • A very good combination. Both may tend to dwell on small hurts, magnifying them out of proportion. But, in general, they are sensitive to each other's needs and get along together well.

Leo • A bad combination. Leo lacks the empathy to divine the mysteries of gentle Pisces. The demanding lion may soon go elsewhere to get attention.

Virgo • An unrewarding relationship. Pisces can open Virgo up, but the process will be long and difficult. It may not be worth the effort, even though Virgo can provide some needed steadiness.

Libra • A tense relationship. Physically, these two are compatible. But when Pisces is looking for someone to depend on, Libra may have just slipped out the back door.

Scorpio • A deeply satisfying relationship. Scorpio needs to possess, and Pisces longs to be possessed. Scorpio can provide all the stability and protection that Pisces craves.

Sagittarius • A disastrous combination. Sagittarius will resent Pisces's emotional needs, and may even mock them. When Sagittarius moves on, Pisces will be left deeply hurt.

Capricorn • A complex relationship. If the goat can accept that there's no way to control Pisces's sudden mood shifts, the relationship can be rewarding.

Aquarius • A very difficult relationship. Pisces is apt to misinterpret Aquarius's actions and imagine the worst. This relationship probably will take more effort than it's worth.

Pisces • A relationship of extremes. When things are going well, they will be in ecstasy. But the slightest provocation can turn them cold and moody.

The text of this book was set in the typeface
Bernhard Modern, and the display was set in
Bernhard Modern Bold by Berryville Graphics
Digital Composition, Berryville, Virginia.

The cover illustration and dingbats through-
out were created by Lisa A. Mahmarian.

Designed   by   Diane   Stevenson/
SNAP • HAUS GRAPHICS. ✴

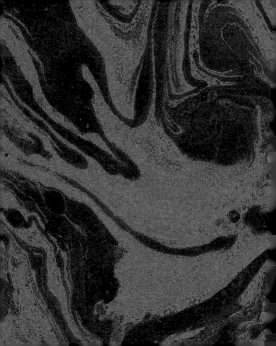